Sincerely His

**I GO TO CHURCH,
I WALKED AN AISLE,
I PRAYED A PRAYER...
"AM I <u>REALLY</u> A CHRISTIAN?"**

By Rob and Lisa Laizure

Copyright © 2004 by Rob and Lisa Laizure

Sincerely His
by Rob and Lisa Laizure

Printed in the United States of America

ISBN 1-594677-80-8

All rights reserved solely by the author. The author guarantees all contents are original and do not infringe upon the legal rights of any other person or work. No part of this book may be reproduced in any form without the permission of the author. The views expressed in this book are not necessarily those of the publisher.

Unless otherwise indicated, all scripture verses are from The MacArthur Study Bible. Copyright © 1997, Word Publishiing. All rights reserved.

The Holy Bible, New King James Version. Copyright © 1979, 1980, 1982 by Thomas Nelson, Inc. Used by permission. all rights reserved.

www.xulonpress.com

PREFACE

From Rob:

Twenty-four years ago in a driveway in Phoenix, I "accepted Christ" into my life—a new Bible, new Jesus stickers on my truck and supposedly a new heart. I was on my way to a new life. I had a new wife, a new job and, as far as I was concerned, I was living the American Dream.

As we settled into our new home and time started to fly, my job became very demanding. Since it took me 5 years to get through high school, I felt I had something to prove, not only to my boss (who happened to be my father), but to myself as well. As I recount those years, I see a pattern of slowly drifting away from that decision I had made about Christ. I stopped reading my Bible and rarely went to church. The ways of the world seemed to attract my attention, which was a far place from where God called this "supposed Christian."

Suddenly the only thing that mattered in my life was money, ego and a huge power trip. My father offered me a promotion, which would devastate one of my brothers, and yet I took it anyway. My life became all about "me." I remember telling my wife that my business was first in my life and she and the kids were second. As I was promoted and the business grew, so did my ego. I felt I could do no wrong. But along with all of this came a home that was suffering deeply. Then my world came tumbling down.

I left my family business position with a six-figure income over a dispute. Because of this decision, we lost our home and my truck, selling everything we had just to keep food on the table, while trying to start our own business. All of my so-called friends seemed to abandon me. It was amazing that as long as I had money, I had all the friends I wanted, but when I was driving a 1980 pickup and selling used baby clothes, the phone stopped ringing.

What a humbling experience but what a growing experience! God used this awful time in my life to make me realize what was important, bringing me full circle back to my wife, children and especially to God. So here is my question. Was I really a Christian when I made that emotional acceptance of Christ 24 years previous? Is it possible that I could make a decision like that and then for the next 15 years lead a life that went against anything that had to do with God?

It was during a very chaotic time in my life about six years ago that I had nowhere to turn. It was then that God reached down and drew me to Himself. I picked up my Bible, started praying again and that was the beginning of what I call my "true conversion." God became the most important part of my life. I only cared to do what He wanted and it has been a continual climb to know Him better each day.

That is what this book is all about. Can a person make a decision like I did and have nothing change? Looking back, I do not think it is possible. As I read God's Word and see that becoming a Christian means becoming a "new man," that the "old man" is gone, I believe that true conversion means true life change. I hope this book will inspire you to do what 2 Corinthians 13:5 says, "Test yourselves to see if you are in the faith; examine yourselves!"

From Lisa:

Am I truly a Christian? These are often unspoken words that so many of us wonder. For me, I "accepted Christ" as a very young child. I was involved with a large Christian organization in high school and by college decided that Christianity had very little to do with the "real world." I would go to church and try to be a good person but that was the extent of my Christian life. I remember one day as I was driving, I actually thought to myself that being a

Christian meant nothing. What had it done to change me in any way? I always felt that God was lucky to have me and He should be very happy that I was smart enough to "accept Him" as a child. I never realized that with those thoughts God was dealing with something much deeper in me. Was I really Christian for those 30 years when I thought I was? What exactly did that mean? For all the crusades that I had seen on TV and all the churches telling me that all I had to do was "go forward" and "receive Christ," it seemed like I did the right thing. But why did it not have any effect on my life?

One Thursday afternoon I heard a pastor speak on, "What it means to be a genuine believer," and I walked out in tears. Was it possible that a person could go to church all her life, believe in Jesus, try to be a good person and yet not truly be saved? That sent me on this little journey to see what God had to say about it. All of my life I just listened and believed that the pastors and preachers I had been listening to were telling me the truth. I didn't need to read the Bible because, even if I did, I'm sure these pastors knew more than I did. I would just believe statements like "once saved, always saved" and never worried about how I lived my life. Was that the truth? Colossians 1:23 says, "If indeed you continue in the faith, grounded and steadfast and are not moved away from the hope of the gospel which you heard...." This verse tells me that I must continue in my faith. It does not say that I will stay stagnant. I used to believe that all I had to do was acknowledge and accept Jesus in my heart and I was in. I was going to heaven because I said a quick prayer one day. But I needed to see if this pastor was telling me the truth, so I decided to pick up the Bible and see what God had to say.

I first had to come to the conclusion that the Bible was truly the Word of God. I had to believe that the Bible was God's way of communicating with His people and when 2 Timothy 3:16 said, "All Scripture is given by inspiration of God, and is profitable for doctrine, for reproof, for instruction in righteousness, that the man of God may be complete, thoroughly equipped for every good work," I had to believe it. If I only took the parts I liked and discounted the rest, then I might as well not read it or believe it at all. Since I do believe that every word in the Bible is inspired by God then I trust what it says about being a Christian.

What I found was truly life changing. Being a Christian was nothing about me, like I had always thought, but it was all about God. It was all about realizing that I was born a sinner and there was a huge gap between God and myself and there was nothing I could do to reach Him. Psalms 51:5 says, "Behold, I was brought forth in iniquity, and in sin my mother conceived me." I could not be good enough or go to church enough or do anything that would please Him. I realized as I read that God is holy and I am sinful. What I learned was that this was never about my "accepting Him," but it was all about His reaching down in grace and mercy and giving me a new life. It was about coming to grips with the fact that I was completely "dead" in my sin and it took an act of God to make me "alive." I started reading verses that said things like, "No one can come to Me unless the Father who sent Me draws him..." (John 6:44) or, "And we know that the Son of God has come and has given us an understanding, that we may know Him who is true...." 1 John 5:20. Then it hit me that God was the instigator of this relationship—not me. He drew me to Him, He told me in Philippians 1:6 that He began a good work in me and would complete it, and in Ezekiel 36:26-27, He said:

> I will give you a new heart and put a new spirit within you; I will take the heart of stone out of your flesh and give you a heart of flesh. I will put My Spirit within you and cause you to walk in My statutes and you will keep My judgments and do them.

Suddenly I understood what it meant to be a Christian and it was the most humbling experience of my life. Instead of this life being about what God could do for me, it became a life of gratitude for what He did do for me. I was bought with a huge price—the blood of Jesus on the cross. And if He bought me with this tremendous price, then I owed Him everything. If I would be spending eternity in heaven with Him then, my life here on earth needed to be lived for Him. Being a Christian never meant saying a short prayer or walking an aisle and I was saved. Could that have been the beginning of my life with Christ? Absolutely. But what would determine that would be what happened after I said that prayer or walked that aisle. Did my life change? Did I love God's Word? Did I spend time talking with Him?

Becoming a Christian is like getting married. When you decide to take that step, your life completely changes. Suddenly your life is not your own any longer. You now have made a decision to live with this person, share a home, live a different lifestyle, and share new responsibilities. The same is true about being a Christian. You made a decision to give your life away to God. You are not a single person doing your own thing anymore but instead you have agreed to share this life with God. With that comes an enormous responsibility to find out what pleases Him and then to live that out. You have made this commitment to Him for "better or worse." Things will never be the same again as you grow together.

These are some of the issues we will deal with in this book. My hope and prayer is that when you are done reading this you will see from God's Word what it really means when you say, "I am a Christian."

TABLE OF CONTENTS

1. What's Sin Got to Do with It?..13
2. But…I'm Religious..19
3. What About My Old Life?..23
4. New Life in Christ 27
5. So What Does It Mean to Say "I Am a Christian"?................31
6. But Church is Boring 41
7. Am I Truly "Heaven Bound"? 45
8. Whose Life Is It Anyway? 47
9. In Conclusion… 49
10. Am I Growing? 53

CHAPTER 1

WHAT'S SIN GOT TO DO WITH IT?

Do I have to understand sin to be a Christian? The answer to this would be a definite yes. The whole idea of being a Christian is that Jesus died on the cross for a specific reason. To understand this we have to go back to the beginning. Sin entered this world when Adam and Eve decided to disobey God. **Romans 5:12 says, "Therefore, just as through one man sin entered the world, and death through sin, and thus death spread to all men, because all sinned...."** Since sin leads to death for all, God had a plan from the beginning of time. In the Old Testament, sins were paid for by animal sacrifices—there had to be blood shed as payment for disobedience to God. **Hebrews 9:22 says, "And according to the law almost all things are purified with blood, and without shedding of blood there is no remission."** The purpose for Jesus was to live a completely sinless life and therefore take our sins upon Himself so we would be holy and blameless in God's sight. **Second Corinthians 5:21 says, "For He made Him who knew no sin to be sin for us, that we might become the righteousness of God in Him."**

In order to be a Christian, the first step would be to understand that I am a sinner in desperate need of a way out. That way was provided by the death and resurrection of Jesus. The problem is that a large majority of churches do not deal with the issue of sin. It is much easier to preach on the love of God or how to be a happy person, but unless the issue of sin is talked about, how can a person come to know Christ? How do I know I need to be saved if I am never told what I need to be saved from? We grew up hearing the phrase "Jesus died on the cross for your sins," which is a completely true statement. But when you understand the depth of that phrase, it is very humbling. What Jesus says in **Matthew 5:3 "Blessed are the poor in spirit, for theirs is the kingdom of heaven,"** is key to becoming a Christian. If I do not come to Christ with the attitude of sheer gratitude and humility, knowing that I would be spending eternity apart from God in a place called hell, then maybe I really don't understand this great exchange—His life for mine, my sins for a life of righteousness. I come to Him broken, knowing that I have no way of getting in a right relationship with God, and yet, because of what Jesus did on the cross, I now have that opportunity.

The problem we have found in people who think they are saved but are not is an enormous sense of pride. We can say that easily enough because we have been in that exact place in our lives. Statements like "I'm a good person," "I go to church each week," "I try to live a moral life," "I'm a nice person," were normal thought patterns for us. Only when we came to the point of realizing that none of those things mattered at all to God but that only a humble, repentant heart did, could our lives begin to change. The dictionary defines pride as: "to high an opinion of one's own ability or worth: a feeling of being better than others" (Copyright 1986 by Merriam-Webster Inc.)

Here's what God has to say about pride:

Psalms 10:4 –
> **"The wicked in his proud countenance does not seek God; God is in none of his thoughts."**

Proverbs 16:5 –
> **"Everyone proud in heart is an abomination to the LORD; though they join forces, none will go unpunished."**

Proverbs 6:16 –
> "These six things the LORD hates, yes, seven are an abomination to Him: a proud look, a lying tongue, hands that shed innocent blood, a heart that devises wicked plans, feet that are swift in running to evil, a false witness who speaks lies, and one who sows discord among brethren."

Psalms 101:5 –
> "Whoever secretly slanders his neighbor, him I will destroy; the one who has a haughty look and a proud heart, him I will not endure."

1 John 2:16 –
> "For all that is in the world—the lust of the flesh, the lust of the eyes, and the pride of life—is not of the Father but is of the world."

James 4:6 –
> "But He gives more grace. Therefore He says: 'God resists the proud, But gives grace to the humble.'"

The dictionary defines being humble like this: "humble - modest or meek in spirit or manner: not proud or bold" (Copyright 1986 by Merriam-Webster Inc.). Here's what God has to say about the humble:

Psalms 138:6 –
> "Though the Lord is on high, yet He regards the lowly; but the proud He knows from afar."

2 Chronicles 34:27 –
> "Because your heart was tender, and you humbled yourself before God when you heard His words against this place and against its inhabitants, and you humbled yourself before Me, and you tore your clothes and wept before Me, I also have heard you,: says the Lord."

Luke 14:11 –
> "For whoever exalts himself will be humbled, and he who humbles himself will be exalted."

James 4:10 –
> "Humble yourselves in the sight of the Lord and He will lift you up."

Matthew 18:4 –
> "Therefore whoever humbles himself as this little child is the greatest in the kingdom of heaven."

Micah 6:8 –
> "He has shown you, O man, what is good; and what does the LORD require of you but to do justly, to love mercy, and the walk humbly with your God"?

In order to come before God truly, we must come with humble hearts. We have to realize that we were born into sin, and to believe anything else is pride. Pride means that we think we are good enough, and as we can see from these verses, God hates pride. His desire is for people to be humble, realizing that it is only through Jesus' paying the penalty for our sins that we can come to Him. Only then can we live holy lives through what Christ has done for us—not what we have done for Him.

Let us do some practical application on what it means to be a sinner. Most people think of sin as the big things that hit the news. Sin means literally "missing the mark." **First John 3:4** explains, **"Whoever commits sin also commits lawlessness, and sin is lawlessness."**

During the course of a day, when was the last time you:

- Raised your voice to your children
- Talked about a co-worker behind his back
- Called in sick to work when you really weren't
- When the phone rang, you told your kids to tell the caller you weren't home

- Found an item at the bottom of your grocery cart and realized you hadn't paid for it and yet you kept it
- Yelled at someone when he cut in front of you in your car in traffic
- Gave someone an evil look when he pulled his cart in front of you at the store
- Were jealous that someone has something that you don't
- Felt sheer hatred for someone who did you wrong
- Wanted to get back at someone for hurting you
- Acted rudely to someone when things didn't go your way
- Reacted with anger toward someone
- Wanted your own way no matter who it hurt
- Gave special attention to someone who you thought could help you climb the corporate ladder
- Had lustful thoughts about someone other than your spouse
- Sat around telling jokes that offended people
- Lied to someone
- Yelled and cursed at your employee
- Took the Lord's name in vain
- Put your hobby in front of spending time worshipping God
- Talked badly about your mother or father
- Wanted something that your neighbor has with a covetous attitude
- Cared more for what you want to do instead of what your spouse or children want?

As you can see, this list could go on forever. There are many people in this world who really do not regard themselves as sinners. **First John 1:8** tells us, **"If we say that we have no sin, we deceive ourselves, and the truth is not in us."** God does not distinguish between little sins and big sins—they are all the same to Him. The horrible crimes that Jeffrey Dahmer committed are no different in God's eyes from the small lies that are told each day. The consequences of these sins are considerably different but each of these are rebellion against God and His laws.

Once we understand the bad news about sin, it is only then that we can get on with the truly great news! That is what "accepting

Christ" is all about. It is accepting the fact that we are sinners and would die in that state if Jesus had not died on the cross to take those sins from us. The first step to becoming a Christian would be to humbly come before Him and admit that we are in desperate need of Him. Only then can we begin our new lives as "Christians."

CHAPTER 2

BUT...I'M RELIGIOUS.

We would say that probably one of the most sobering verses in the Bible is found in **Matthew 7:21:**

> **Not everyone who says to Me "Lord, Lord," shall enter the kingdom of heaven, but he who does the will of my Father in heaven. Many will say to Me in that day, 'Lord, Lord, have we not prophesied in Your name, cast out demons in your name, and done many wonders in your name?' And then I will declare to them, 'I never knew you; depart from Me, you who practice lawlessness!'"**

To understand this verse we have to distinguish what the word "knew" means. Does God know everyone? Yes, but not everyone in the same sense. To be a Christian is to be known by God in a very intimate, personal way. It is not a shallow relationship. You may have a lot of friends that you "know," but the relationship you have with your spouse is different. There is that true sense of "knowing" that person that is different from any other relationship.

This is a very difficult verse because what it shows us is that there are many people doing very religious deeds and yet Jesus says He never knew them. There seems to be this opinion that as long as you go to church once a week, throw a little money in the offering and be as nice as you can during the week, then that would constitute your being a Christian. When Jesus says that He will tell these people to depart from Him, this should throw a big warning flag in front of us. Are we busy doing God's work, involved in the choir, or teaching a Bible study, and yet doing it for all the wrong reasons? If God has given you the gift to do any one of these things, they should be done with an enormous sense of humility. Are you studying so that you can teach others humbly or do you feel a sense of pride for knowing so much? Are you singing in the choir because you feel like you have a great voice that everyone needs to hear, or is the only reason you are singing because you know your voice is a gift from God and you want to use it for Him? There is a huge difference between being religious and working for the Lord out of a grateful, humble heart.

The Pharisees were a group of very religious men in the New Testament. They prayed the longest and the loudest, they gave the money that was expected of them, they tried to keep all of the law. If that were what mattered to God, then they would be the first to get into heaven! But that isn't what matters to God. Here is what Jesus had to say about all their religious activity. **Matthew 23:13 "But woe to you, scribes and Pharisees, hypocrites! For you shut up the kingdom of heaven against men; for you neither go in yourselves, nor do you allow those who are entering to go in."** For all of their religious activity, Jesus said they were not going to heaven. So what's the deal? If we pray, go to church and give money and that doesn't make us a Christian, then what does? Religion certainly doesn't, but a relationship with the God of the universe through Jesus Christ does.

Another pervasive thought is that it doesn't matter what you believe in as long as you just believe. This is where we have to go back to what the Bible says. **John 14:6** states, **"Jesus said to him, 'I am the way, the truth, and the life. No one comes to the Father except through Me.'"** Acts 4:12 says, **"Nor is there salvation in any other, for there is no other name under heaven given among men by which we must be saved."** The point is that if you are basing your Christianity on your denomination or your church membership, then this might be a good time to reflect on why you do consider yourself a Christian. Religion is man's attempt to reach God through tradition, rules and regulations, or keeping the law. When Jesus says that He is the only way to God, it doesn't matter what religious activity you are doing. If you are not basing your Christianity on Jesus and His blood on the cross to wash away your sins, then the Bible says that you are not a Christian.

CHAPTER 3

WHAT ABOUT MY OLD LIFE?

First, let's talk about the old life. This would be the life you lived before you came to know Christ in a personal way. Take a look at what the Bible says about the old man and your old life.

Do you love yourself more than God and what He wants you to be? Do you care more about making money and spending money than you do about God? Do you brag to people about your golf scores or the new car you're going to get? Do you take an irreverent attitude about God? Do you see Him as holy or just "the man upstairs"? Do you obey your parents? Are you grateful for the things you have in your life? When people outside the church see your life, do they see a life that would be considered holy? Do your co-workers or employees see a holy attitude at work? Do you love people that are not easy to love? Do you love your enemies and the people who have clearly hurt you? Have you forgiven the person who has done you wrong? Have you said anything bad about someone when they weren't around? Have you yelled at someone? Have you wanted your own way without regard for the other person? When was the last time you let someone have his own way even if you thought he were wrong? Has spending time on your hobbies on Sunday become a norm rather than an exception?

The previous questions and the following verses should help us see if we truly do have a new life or are still living the old one.

2 Timothy 3:2 –
> "For men will be lovers of themselves, lovers of money, boasters, proud, blasphemers, disobedient to parents, unthankful, unholy, unloving, unforgiving, slanderers, without self-control, brutal, despisers of good, traitors, headstrong, haughty, lovers of pleasure rather than lovers of God."

Colossians 3:5-6 –
> "Therefore put to death your members which are on the earth: fornication, uncleanness, passion, evil desire and covetousness, which is idolatry. Because of these things the wrath of God is coming upon the sons of disobedience in which you yourselves ONCE WALKED when you lived in them." (Emphasis ours.)

Colossians 3:8 –
> "But now you yourselves are to put off all these: anger, wrath, malice, blasphemy, filthy language out of your mouth. Do not lie to one another, since you have put off the old man with his deeds, and have put on the new man who is renewed in knowledge according to the image of Him who created him."

1 Corinthians 6:9 –
> "Do you not know that the unrighteous will not inherit the kingdom of God? Do not be deceived. Neither fornicators, nor idolaters, nor adulterers, nor homosexuals, nor sodomites, nor thieves, nor covetous, nor drunkards, nor revilers, nor extortioners will inherit the kingdom of God. And such WERE some of you. But you were washed, but you were sanctified, but you were justified in the name of the Lord Jesus and by the Spirit of our God."

1 Peter 2:1 –
"Therefore, laying aside all malice, all deceit, hypocrisy, envy and all evil speaking...."

Romans 1:29 –
"Being filled with all unrighteousness, sexual immorality, wickedness, covetousness, maliciousness; full of envy, murder, strife, deceit, evil-mindedness; they are whisperers...."

Jeremiah 9:5 –
"Everyone will deceive his neighbor and will not speak the truth; they have taught their tongue to speak lies; they weary themselves to commit iniquity."

1 Timothy 5:13 –
"And besides they learn to be idle, wandering about from house to house, and not only idle but also gossips and busybodies, saying things which they ought not."

1 John 2:11 –
"But he who hates his brother is in darkness and walks in darkness, and does not know where he is going, because the darkness has blinded his eyes."

Titus 3:3 –
"For we ourselves were also once foolish, disobedient, deceived, serving various lusts and pleasures, living in malice and envy, hateful and hating one another."

John 3:19 –
"And this is the condemnation, that the light has come in to the world and men loved darkness rather that light because their deeds were evil."

As you can see from these verses, mostly a sheer selfish attitude and one that is all about "me, myself, and I" characterize the old life. There doesn't seem to be any recognition of humility and wanting to spend time with or to please God. The old life consisted of living in darkness, void of any light. Now that we have seen what characterizes the old life and the old man, let's turn to see what this wonderful new life in Christ is all about.

CHAPTER 4

NEW LIFE IN CHRIST

How can we begin to understand what this "new life" looks like? This is especially hard in the culture that we live in today. We have so many churches that want to build our self-esteem, make sure we are comfortable in our pews and never want to upset us. They seldom talk about sin; they talk only of God's love without the balance of His wrath, and the compromise goes on. The Christian life is not about always being happy but it is about being joyful. As we read through the Bible, we see Christians being beaten, persecuted, stoned, and imprisoned. We see that being a Christian means you are living like a foreigner in a different country. We see being a Christian means living a life that goes in direct conflict with what the world thinks. Being a Christian means loving the things that God loves and hating the things He hates. Being a Christian means living a life that contradicts the world system in which we live. Being a Christian means reading His Word and living it.

Here are some examples of what the Bible says a Christian is.

Matthew 5:14 –
> **"You are the light of the world. A city that is set on a hill cannot be hidden."**

1 John 2:15 –
> "Do not love the world or the things in the world. If anyone loves the world, the love of the Father is not in Him."

1 John 1:6 –
> "If we say that we have fellowship with Him, and walk in darkness, we lie and do not practice the truth."

1 John 2:6 –
> "He who says he abides in Him ought himself also to walk just as He walked."

1 Corinthians 10:31 –
> "Therefore, whether you eat or drink or whatever you do, do all to the glory of God."

Galatians 5:22 –
> "But the fruit of the Spirit is love, joy, peace longsuffering, kindness, goodness, faithfulness, gentleness, self-control."

Ephesians 1:4 –
> "Just as He chose us in Him before the foundation of the world, that we should be holy and without blame before Him."

Ephesians 2:10 –
> "For we are His workmanship, created in Christ Jesus for good works, which God prepared beforehand that we should walk in them."

Philippians 1:29 –
> "For to you it has been granted on behalf of Christ, not only to believe in Him but also to suffer for His sake."

Matthew 6:19 –
> "Do not lay up for yourselves treasures on earth, where moth and rust destroy and where thieves break in and steal; but lay up for yourselves treasures in heaven, where neither moth nor rust destroys and where thieves do not break in and steal."

Matthew 10:38 –
> "And he who does not take his cross and follow after Me is not worthy of Me."

Matthew 10:39 –
> "He who finds his life will lose it, and he who loses his life for My sake will find it."

Colossians 3:1 –
> "If then you were raised with Christ seek those things which are above where Christ is, sitting at the right hand of God. Set your mind on things above, not on things on the earth."

Colossians 3:12 –
> "Therefore, as the elect of God, holy and beloved, put on tender mercies, kindness, humility, meekness, longsuffering; bearing with one another and forgiving one another, if anyone has a complaint against another; even as Christ forgave you, so you also must do."

2 Timothy 2:15 –
> "Be diligent to present yourself approved to God, a worker who does not need to be ashamed, rightly dividing the word of truth."

This list could go on and on, but hopefully you are seeing a pattern. This Christian life is not about what is going to make you comfortable. This Christian life is about living your life as a servant to Christ and others. He died for you and you live for Him.

Some of the churches in our day are trying desperately to "win people to Jesus" by telling them that they will get whatever they want if they come to Him. These churches are promising wealth and prosperity if they would give their lives to Christ. Some are promising happiness; some are promising health. To be a Christian is to realize that none of those things matter. To be a Christian is not for personal gain or what one can get out of this. To be a Christian is living with an attitude of gratefulness and thanksgiving that through Jesus we have been saved from our lives of sin. When I truly give my life to Christ I am exchanging my old life of sin and disobedience for a new life of pleasing God. With that comes an unbelievable amount of joy and peace.

Joy and peace is what God promises. He promises that when you go through trials, it is for your own good—to help you grow stronger and trust Him more. **James 1:2-3 says, "My brethren, count it all joy when you fall into various trials, knowing that the testing of your faith produces patience. But let patience have its perfect work, that you may be perfect and complete, lacking nothing."** When you look at the life of Paul in the Bible you will see that he had a "thorn in the flesh." In **2 Corinthians 12:9** he asked God three times to remove it and God said no, **"my grace is sufficient for you."** Being a Christian means trusting your life to God. When good things happen, you rejoice; when bad things happen, you also rejoice. Why? Because you have the peace and assurance that your life is in His hands and **Romans 8:28** says **that "all things work together for the good, for those who love God."**

So what is this new life? **Colossians 1:13** says, **"He has delivered us from the power of darkness and conveyed us into the kingdom of the Son of His love, In whom we have redemption through His blood, the forgiveness of sins."** What a great concept! We were in darkness and God delivered us and gave us this new life.

CHAPTER 5

SO WHAT DOES IT MEAN TO SAY "I AM A CHRISTIAN"?

Now that we have determined that being a Christian does not mean religious activity, checking a box or walking an aisle, then what does it mean to say "I am a Christian"? Our first response would be to say there has to be a life change. To be a Christian means first to realize you are a sinner in need of a Savior, and then to give your life to Him. Change does not happen overnight but it is virtually impossible to say you are a Christian and yet have no life change at all. **Ezekiel 36:26** says:

> **"I will give you a new heart and put a new spirit within you; I will take the heart of stone out of your flesh and give you a heart of flesh. I will put My Spirit within you and cause you to walk in My statutes, and you will keep My judgments and do them."**

If God puts this new heart in you, then your life will start to look like His. When you come to grips with the fact that you were completely dead in sin and God in His grace and mercy made you alive and has given you a new life, then the only appropriate response is love and gratitude. **Ephesians 2:8** says, **"For by grace**

you have been saved through faith, and that not of yourselves; it is the gift of God." Your life begins to change when you understand that you are a believer because God has graciously given this gift to you. This knowledge begins to promote a lifestyle that truly reflects what it looks like to be a believer.

The first part to being a Christian is something called repentance. All through the Bible we are called to repent, which means to turn away from sin. **2 Corinthians 7:10 says, "For godly sorrow produces repentance leading to salvation, not to be regretted; but the sorrow of the world produces death."** When someone who is not a Christian gets caught in sin he tends to feel badly about what he did, but mostly he feels badly because he got caught. But to the Christian, when he is caught in sin, there is a godly sorrow – one that breaks his heart because he has sinned against God. Because of his love for Him, he turns from his sin, and the key is that he works to try and not do it again. Not because of rules and regulations like the Pharisees, but because he loves being in fellowship with God and he knows until he repents, he won't have that close relationship with Him.

Why are our churches not preaching true repentance? The churches today are doing a grave disservice to the people in their congregations. The entire Gospel is about repenting and the forgiveness of sins through Jesus. If we are not being taught that true repentance follows faith in Christ, then we are not being taught what the Bible is all about. We need to make a point very clear here. You are not in a right standing with God because of your repentant lifestyle. You have a repentant lifestyle because of your faith in Christ. It cannot be backwards or you would be basing your salvation on working your way to God. *A repentant lifestyle is evidence of your faith.*

When you truly become a Christian God begins a life long work in your life. **Philippians 1:6 says, "...being confident of this very thing, that He who has begun a good work in you will complete it until the day of Jesus Christ."** This work does not happen in a day, a month, or a year. God is working in our lives to remove the sin and replace it with righteous living. He gives us a desire to live a holy life through continual repentance. When we become Christians our lives should look a lot different this year than last year. If you are not seeing any change or growth spiritually from year to year, then this is also a time to question if you truly are a Christian.

Will we ever live a sin-free life? Absolutely not! There will always be a constant battle between sinful desires and actions, but because of our love for Christ, we start desiring holiness over sin. Being a Christian means that for all the sin that still remains in our lives we will never be condemned for them. **Romans 8:1** says, **"There is therefore now no condemnation to those who are in Christ Jesus, who do not walk according to the flesh, but according to the Spirit."** But that never gives us a reason to continue to sin. In fact, because of the knowledge that we are not condemned should only invoke a repentant heart.

Repentance is hard because that means you have to first confess to God that you have disobeyed Him. **1 John 1:9** says, **"If we confess our sins, He is faithful and just to forgive us our sins and to cleanse us from all unrighteousness."** When we get angry with our kids, employees, employers, friends or family and know that it is uncalled for, then our first reaction is to confess to God and apologize to the person offended. Because you love God you want to please Him means you need to be reading His Word to see what He requires of you. When the Bible says love is patient and you are impatient with your spouse, you need to confess and repent. When you are rude to someone where you work, you need to confess and repent. The more you do this, the more you will think twice before you are impatient or rude. This would be a good time to go back to the list in the chapter "What's Sin Got to Do With It?" When you do these things in your everyday life, do you confess to God? Do you apologize to the person you have offended? Do you turn from that behavior? These are the true fruits of repentance.

The second thing that happens when a person comes to Christ is he wants to learn all he can. Suddenly he has this need to understand why he believes, what he believes, how he should live, and how he can tell others. The only way that will happen is to read God's Word—the Bible. When a person falls in love, the first thing that happens is he wants to spend as much time as possible with the object of his love. That is what happens when you become a Christian.

Suddenly there doesn't seem to be enough time in the day to learn. **Psalm 63:1** says, **"O God, You are my God; early will I seek You; my soul thirsts for You; my flesh longs for You in a dry and thirsty land."** There is this desire to know this God who sent His Son to die in your place so that you could spend eternity with Him.

In this day and age of technology, there is never a reason not to read the Bible. You can read it in book form, over the Internet, or in many forms of audio. The problem is that most people do not know where to begin, so they skip around and none of it makes sense.

Our suggestion would be to buy a One Year Daily Bible at a Christian bookstore. We as Christians need to be reading through the Bible each and every year of our lives. We will never know how God calls us to live if we are not studying His Word. Many Christians feel that reading the Bible through once is enough for a lifetime and yet the more we read, the more we grow. Our challenge to you would be to read different translations each year, starting with the New Living Translation and then the next year going to the New International Version. Studying the Bible is not a one-time project—it is a lifetime project.

The best advice we ever got was from a tape series by John MacArthur. He recommends you take a small book in the Bible like 1 John, which has 5 chapters. Read those same 5 chapters each day for 30 days. By the end of those 30 days, you will have a great insight on who God is and how He expects us to live. After those 30 days, start with the book of John. Read 5 chapters a day for the next 30 days. In about 4 months, you will know all about the life of Jesus. Try to do this through the New Testament. It would take about 15 minutes a day to do this and you will be amazed at what you learn. When you realize that the Bible is the way God communicates to us, then it makes it all the more valuable.

If you do not feel a need or desire to read the Bible, I would challenge you to start today. God has so much to say to you and you will never know His heart if you don't spend the time with Him. There are days we wake up and really don't have the desire to read. But it is on those days that we read out of obedience. You will be amazed at what you can learn on the days that you don't feel like reading. **Luke 11:28** says, **"But He said, 'More than that, blessed** are those that hear the Word of God and keep it.'" The question would be how could we keep God's Word if we don't know what it says? This takes a commitment to wake up a little earlier or stay up a little later. For a person who claims to be a Christian, this is the most natural thing to do. This becomes a huge part of your life because the only way to get to know God is to read and study about Him. If you say you are a Christian and never read your Bible, you need to spend some time questioning if, in fact, you really do have a relationship with Christ. **2 Chronicles 15:2** says, **"...If you seek Him, He will be found by you; but if you forsake Him, He will forsake you."**

It is so important to read and study the Bible. One good reason would be to make sure that what you are being taught is the truth. When you come to the realization that the Bible is God's Word to us, then regardless of what it says, we are to obey. Unfortunately, in many pulpits today, pastors are making the Bible say whatever they want. Instead of studying the historical, grammatical, and literal meaning, the Bible is preached out of context a lot of the time. If you are reading daily and you come up with something you do not understand, then study it. We were working through an issue and we went to four different pastors for their answers. All of them gave us different answers! If you get nothing else from this book, this would be the most important. Please, do not just believe a pastor because he is a pastor or a Christian because you assume he knows more than you. Study for yourself. Read the Bible yourself. The Bible is really not that hard to understand. If you have a problem with a verse then you need to find other verses that will help you interpret the meaning. It just takes time and effort and, for the person who is truly a Christian, it is a vitally important part of his life.

Please remember this. You must take the Bible at face value and take it as the ONLY authority. God never intended for books to be added or doctrines to be added or traditions to take the place of God's Word. God takes adding to or subtracting from the Bible very seriously, as it says in **Revelation 22:18-19**:

> **For I testify to everyone who hears the words of the prophecy of this book: If anyone adds to these**

> **things, God will add to him the plagues that are written in this book; and if anyone takes away from the words of the book of this prophecy, God shall take away his part from the Book of Life, from the holy city, and *from* the things which are written in this book.**

When you are facing a situation, it doesn't matter what you feel. It only matters what God has to say about it. If you are considering a divorce and all your friends think that would be the right thing to do, what does the Bible say? That is where the obedience to the Scriptures comes in. It doesn't matter what your friends think; it only matters what God thinks. You are called to be obedient to God's Word only—not your church, not your pastor, not your tradition. When you truly become a Christian, you will live your life based on only what God has to say.

There is also a flip side to this. There are many people today that do know a lot about the Bible. They know Bible history, can quote verse after verse and have an enormous amount of knowledge. But please remember our friends the Pharisees, the pious religious leaders of Jesus' day. They knew more than anyone about the Law and what God's word said but they didn't know how to put it into practice. This is also another red flag. *The fruit of knowledge is shown in how you live what you have learned.*

The third part to being a Christian is holiness. We should continually strive as Christians to live holy lives. The problem today is that many Christians do not know what that means. Unfortunately a lot of churches are more concerned about making you comfortable than teaching you about holiness. When you read the Bible and start seeing the holiness of God, it is amazing how that will affect your life. **First Peter 1:15** says:

> **But as He who called you is holy, you also be holy in all your conduct." Romans 6:13 says, "And do not present your members as instruments of unrighteousness to sin, but present yourselves to God as being alive from the dead, and your**

members as instruments of righteousness to God.

As a new Christian the world has to see a difference. **2 Corinthians 5:17** explains:

"Therefore, if anyone is in Christ, he is a new creation; old things have passed away; behold, all things have become new." Ephesians 4:24 emphasis, **"...and that you put on the new man which was created according to God, in true righteousness and holiness."**

The problem today is that many churches will not take a stand on holy living for fear of alienating people. The Bible is very clear that to be a Christian is to live a holy, godly life. If you were truly a Christian, any unholy living would produce true repentance.

How many times have you heard of someone who refuses to go to church because they feel the churches are filled with hypocrites? Unfortunately, there are many people who refuse to come to Christ based on knowing someone who claims to be a Christian but refuses to live like one. If your boss claims to be a Christian and yet in the work place he yells, swears and is unkind, how can those actions possibly promote Christianity? If your friend claims to be a Christian and yet spends her time gossiping about other people, does that make you want to know Christ? If you claim to be a Christian, can unbelievers distinguish that you truly are by how you talk? What about at the club, on the golf course, hunting or fishing? What do you talk about at lunch with the girls, at the nail salon or when you get your hair done? Do your words and actions show that you truly are a Christian? **James 1:22** tells us, **"But be doers of the word, and not hearer only, deceiving yourselves." Colossians 4:6** says **"Let your speech always be with grace, seasoned with salt, that you may know how you ought to answer each one."**

The word "Christian" is thrown around like it is a synonym for being American. The problem is that people do not realize that if they do not have a GENUINE knowledge of Him, which only comes from reading His Word, then they probably are not Christians. You have to know whom you believe in before you can truly believe.

Here is the bottom line. *You can talk about God, pretend to know God, but if your life does not reflect God, you probably are not a Christian.* When a person truly comes to know Christ, it changes everything. The way you think, the way you act, and how you treat people are all evidence of a truly changed life. Either we have to make a decision to live for Him and be worthy of the calling in which He has called us or we need to walk away and quit pretending to believe something that we refuse to live.

Galatians 2:20 says, "I have been crucified with Christ; it is no longer I who live, but Christ lives in me; and the life which I now live in the flesh I live by faith in the Son of God, who loved me and gave Himself for me."

Hopefully this is all coming together for you. Being a Christian does not mean saying a quick prayer of "accepting Christ" at some point in your life. That could have been the defining moment when your Christian life began, but only time will tell if it was a true or false conversion. This book was written for the many people who believe that saying a quick prayer to "receive Christ" will catapult them straight to heaven. As you can see from what the Bible says, that is not the truth. **Matthew 7:13 admonishes us: "Enter by the narrow gate; for wide is the gate and broad is the way that leads to destruction, and there are many who go in by it. Because narrow is the gate and difficult is the way which leads to life, and there are few who find it."**

Saying a quick prayer or walking an aisle does not seem to be the difficult way that the Bible talks about. If a church is preaching this as the truth then they are preaching false doctrine. Once you spend time reading the Bible, you will see that the Christian life is not easy. Full of joy? Absolutely, but not easy. Friends, family and co-workers will laugh at you for your beliefs. You will lose friends when your lifestyle changes. People will think you are crazy when you stop living in sin. The Christian life is a life lived to please God. **Colossians 1:10 explains: "That you may walk worthy of**

the Lord, fully pleasing Him, being fruitful in every good work and increasing in the knowledge of God." And **Colossians 3:1** adds, **"It is "seek the things which are above, not things that are on this earth"**

Prayerfully analyzing each scripture is essential. For example, read **1 Corinthians 13, verses 4-7** in the Bible. How do we live this passage? When it says **"love is patient and kind, never jealous or envious, never haughty or selfish or rude, that love does not seek its own, is not easily provoked and thinks no evil"**—what is the application? In every relationship you start to measure how you treat people by these verses. About that co-worker who got a promotion, are you jealous and envious, or to your spouse who woke up grouchy, are you kind? When you want to go out for steak and your family wants pizza, are you annoyed? When you don't get your own way, are you angry?

The Bible has so many answers on how a Christian should act and respond in different situations. Christianity is life changing. It means loving God with all your heart, soul, and mind, being in His Word daily to see how He wants you to live and living it, and then sharing your new life with others.

CHAPTER 6

BUT CHURCH IS BORING

We hear so many excuses why people do not go to church. They think it is boring, they don't get anything out of it, it is their only day to sleep in, or it wastes part of their day. For a Christian, going to church is probably the best day of the week. After you give your life to Christ you have this huge desire to worship Him and honor Him. You have this desire to learn what God has to say from His Word. You have this desire to be around other believers who feel the same way as you do. Going to church is a humbling time of grateful thanksgiving to the God who saved us from eternal separation from Him.

Unfortunately, church has become like the theater. The productions are grand, the singing spectacular, and the preaching always lets you walk out feeling content and comfortable about yourself. Churches have become a social gathering. When joining the church softball league is more important than learning God's Word, then there is a big problem!

The sermons are short for fear of "boring" the congregation. Let's look and see what the Bible says about what should be going on in church. **Second Timothy 4:2-5** says:

> **Preach the Word! Be ready in season and out of season. Convince, rebuke, exhort with all longsuffering and teaching. For the time will come when**

> **they will not endure sound doctrine, but according to their own desires, because they have itching ears, they will heap up for themselves teachers; and they will turn their ears away from the truth, and be turned aside to fables. But you be watchful in all things, endure afflictions, do the work of an evangelist, fulfill your ministry.**

As a new Christian the first thing you need to do is find a true, Bible teaching church. As you can see from this verse, the Bible makes it very clear that you need to be in a place where God's Word is being taught. So many churches today are compromising the Word for fear of losing their members. If they actually taught what the Bible says on issues like homosexuality, abortion, pre-marital sex, or divorce, there might be that chance of offending someone. Many churches refuse to take a stand on certain issues, and yet if the Bible does, then the churches must also.

Our suggestion would be to find a church that preaches through the Bible verse by verse. This is called expository preaching. Because the Bible says to "preach the Word," we are convinced this is so important to your growth as a Christian. Unfortunately, many churches today are trying so desperately to make people feel comfortable, the sermons tend to be mostly about you with a little God thrown in. As Christians our goal in life is to do everything to the glory of God. We need to care only about God's opinion, and that can only be understood by hearing God's Word taught.

Look for a church that isn't trying to look like the world. So many of the large churches today are afraid to offend anyone so they tend to preach only what they think you want to hear. Any talk of sin or repentance is usually not found for fear of alienating or hurting someone's feelings. The Bible states that the church is to "convince, exhort and rebuke" "Convince" means to show someone the error of their behavior. "Rebuke" means to deal with someone's sin and lead them to repentance. A person cannot truly come to know Christ and live a godly life if they are not being taught biblical principles.

If you go to a church that only preaches about God's love then you might want to consider a new church. Is God love? Absolutely. But that would be a small part of the Gospel. A church has to tell you about sin, God's wrath, and that you will be eternally separated to a place called "hell" if you do not repent.

People have to be taught about God's love and mercy and grace so they can know what Jesus is all about. How can a person truly be a Christian if they don't even know what the whole Bible says? It is the church's responsibility to tell you "the truth, the whole truth and nothing but the truth." We urge you to find a church with these qualities and you will as **Colossians 1:10** says, **"...walk worthy of the Lord, fully pleasing Him, being fruitful in every good work and INCREASING IN THE KNOWLEDGE OF GOD...."** (Emphasis ours.)

CHAPTER 7

AM I TRULY "HEAVEN BOUND?"

Assurance of your salvation is something Christians seem to struggle with all the time. But as a Christian, that should never be an issue. When you truly become a Christian, God puts His Spirit within you and your life changes. Your life is now in a growth pattern. As you learn what the Bible says, you fall more deeply in love with this God who created you, who drew you to Himself, and who paid the penalty for your sins so that you could spend eternal life with Him in heaven forever.

As you read and familiarize yourself with the Bible you will start seeing that there is nothing you can do to earn your way to heaven but that your salvation is based on what Jesus did for you.

> **2 Timothy 1:9** tells us, "...who has saved us and called us with a holy calling, not according to our works, but according to His own purpose and grace which was given to us in Christ Jesus before time began."

> **John 10:28-29** says, "And I give them eternal life, and they shall never perish; neither shall anyone snatch them out of my hand. My Father, who has given them to Me, is greater than all; and no one is able to snatch them out of My Father's hand."

If God has called us and given us this new life and He promises that nobody will snatch us out of His hand—that would be reason enough to be assured. So many "religions" today base salvation on what you can do for God. Have you done enough good deeds today? Have you given enough money today? Have you prayed enough today? How much is enough? What a frightening way to spend this wonderful life that God has given us. Our salvation is based on putting our faith and trust in Him—knowing we could never be good enough. Our salvation is based on what Jesus did on the cross—not on anything we do for Him. **Ephesians 2:8-9** says:

> **For by grace you have been saved through faith, and that not of yourselves;** *it is* **the gift of God, not of works, lest anyone should boast. 10 For we are His workmanship, created in Christ Jesus for good works, which God prepared beforehand that we should walk in them.**

Only when we realize this can we truly come to know what it means to be assured of our salvation.

Once you come to terms with this, assurance of your salvation becomes natural. When you come to Christ in true repentance and true faith and your life begins to change and you love God's Word and love to fellowship with other believers, then you can have the confidence that you truly are a believer. If you are basing your salvation on any of your works or deeds then you should stop and question yourself. If you think you're a "good" person or a "nice" person or a "moral" person and you think you are going to heaven because of those things, you need to step back and realize you are believing something that the Bible does not say. Remember, it is only our trust and faith in Jesus that saves us and gives us the assurance that we will spend eternity with Him forever. We are assured of this in **1 John 5:11-12: "And this is the testimony: that God has given us eternal life, and this life is in His Son. He who has the Son has life; he who does not have the Son of God does not have life."**

CHAPTER 8

WHOSE LIFE IS IT, ANYWAY?

When a person truly comes to know Christ, there comes a realization that you are no longer your own person. When you realize the magnitude of what it means to be a Christian, you come to the knowledge that you have given up the rights to your life to Christ. That permeates every area of your life. Work takes on a different meaning since you are to do everything "to the glory of God." Your hobbies take on a different meaning since they become secondary to serving God and others. Your school takes on a different meaning since you are there to be a "light" to others. Your home life changes because you learn how God calls you to treat your spouse and family. Your relationships change because God tells you to "love one another," and "love your enemies." Your thinking changes. Things that used to matter suddenly don't. Instead of always looking at the temporal you put more emphasis on the eternal. Our pastor once said that God changes your "wanter." The things you used to want to do you suddenly don't want to do anymore!

What a great way to live! God is moving in your life to make and mold you into the kind of person He wants you to be. He called you for a purpose and now He is moving your heart to desire the things He desires. He is replacing all of the old habits with things that please Him. He is taking your life and making it His.

CHAPTER 9

IN CONCLUSION...

This book has been written as a plea for all the people who believe they are Christians to take an inventory of their lives. When the Bible says in **2 Corinthians 13:5, "Examine yourselves as to whether you are in the faith. Test yourselves...,"** we take that very seriously. We are concerned for the many people who have been taught that walking an aisle or checking a box will save them. We are concerned with the people who believe they are Christians yet continue to live their lives the way they want. We are concerned because we were once among them. What has dramatically changed our lives are a few verses:

Ephesians 1:4 –
> "...just as He chose us in Him before the foundation of the world, that we should be holy and without blame before Him in love, having predestined us to adoption as sons by Jesus Christ to Himself, according to the good pleasure of His will...."

Ephesians 2:10 –
> "For we are His workmanship, created in Christ Jesus for good works, which God prepared beforehand that we should walk in them."

John 6:44 –
> **"No one can come to Me unless the Father who sent Me draws Him; and I will raise Him up at the last day."**

Once we came to the realization that we are Christians today because God drew us to Himself, chose us for Himself and created us for good works, then our lives took on a new meaning. Instead of feeling that God was lucky that we chose Him, we became very humble, realizing that He chose us. We became very humble, realizing that we would spend eternity in heaven with God because of His instigating this relationship. When **Matthew 7:13-14** says, **"Enter by the narrow gate; for wide is the gate and broad is the way that leads to destruction, and there are many who go in by it. Because narrow is the gate and difficult is the way which leads to life and there are FEW who find it."** (Emphasis ours.) The narrow gate means humbly coming to Jesus and turning your life over to Him. It is humbly realizing you are a sinner and in desperate need of being forgiven, changing your life according to His standards, and becoming a new person. It is a narrow way but it is the only way.

So, in conclusion, our prayer is that you would look at your lives and measure them by what the Bible says are the true characteristics of a Christian. Remember, we are not talking about religion or religious activity. We are not talking about the church you go to or the traditions to which you cling. We are talking about three kinds of people.

1. TRUE CHRISTIANS: If you humbly come before God in repentance and faith, trusting in what Jesus did for you on the cross, love His Word, love to worship Him and seek to live a holy life and persevere to the end, then you can be assured that you are a Christian.

2. BABY CHRISTIANS: If you have just decided to give your life to Christ and understand the meaning of that—welcome to the family! You are in for the most joyful ride of your life! Just because you are a Christian does not mean that everything will always go your way. But as you read God's Word and get to know the God who saved you, you will have the peace and assurance that you can

trust Him with your life. That means good times and bad times. He is working all things for good and you can live a joyous and peaceful life knowing that.

3. NOT CHRISTIANS: If, on the other hand, you read this book and realize that you do not think you are a sinful person, you never or seldom pick up and study the Bible, rarely go to church and never think about living a holy life that pleases God, then you need to take a sincere look at whether you truly are a Christian.

If you are basing your Christianity on church membership, a walk down the aisle, a check in the box, or a quick prayer "accepting Christ" without any growth spiritually in your life, then you need to question if you are "truly in the faith." Our suggestion is to that you spend some time seeking God, reading His Word everyday and finding a sound Bible-teaching church. <u>Ask God to give you a heart to seek Him.</u> Ask Him to show you what a true Christian looks like. And remember and have confidence in the fact that **John 6:37** says, **"All that the Father gives Me will come to Me, and the one who comes to Me I will by no means cast out."**

CHAPTER 10

AM I GROWING?

The last chapter of this book is for those who are Christians. This part of the book was meant as a challenge. Please remember that when we first give our lives to Jesus, the Holy Spirit comes into our lives. This is affirmed in Ezekiel 36:27: **"I will put My Spirit within you and cause you to walk in My statutes, and you will keep My judgments and do *them*."** It is up to Him to convict us of our sin and change our lives. As you ask yourself these questions, pray that God would change those areas that need to be changed and thank Him for those areas that He has already worked on.

Remember, being a Christian is a life-long process! Some areas will take longer to change than others but there should be some evidence of change each year. Use these questions to see how relevant the Bible is to our everyday lives. God wants our lives to look like His Son's life, but that only happens by reading the Bible, repenting of what God shows us is wrong, and continuing on. God promises in **Philippians 1:6 that "He who began a good work in you will continue it until the day of Christ Jesus."** What a promise that is to us! May that promise help us persevere and continue on as we study to live our lives "sincerely" for Him.

THE ONLY WAY TO SALVATION

1. Do you understand that God has made it possible through Christ to be saved?

Matthew 19:25-26 –
"When His disciples heard it, they were greatly astonished, saying, 'Who then can be saved?' But Jesus looked at them and said to them, 'With men this is impossible, but with God all things are possible.'"

Acts 4:12 –
"Nor is there salvation in any other, for there is no other name under heaven given among men by which we must be saved."

John 14:6 –
"Jesus said to him, 'I am the way, the truth, and the life. No one comes to the Father except through Me.'"

2. Do you understand that to be a child of God means we must be born again? We are given a new start and continue to grow just as a child grows.

John 1:12-13 –
"But as many as received Him, to them He gave the right to become children of God, to those who believe in His name: 13 who were born, not of blood, nor of the will of the flesh, nor of the will of man, but of God."

John 3:3 –
"Jesus answered and said to him, "Most assuredly, I say to you, unless one is born again, he cannot see the kingdom of God."

3. Do you understand that to believe means more than just being knowledgeable about something? Do you see that it means there

must be a change in your life because of what you believe?

James 1:22-24 –
>"But be doers of the word, and not hearers only, deceiving yourselves. For if anyone is a hearer of the word and not a doer, he is like a man observing his natural face in a mirror; for he observes himself, goes away, and immediately forgets what kind of man he was."

4. Are you ashamed of the Gospel? Do you understand that it is the only way that people can become saved?

Romans 1:16 –
>"For I am not ashamed of the gospel of Christ, for it is the power of God to salvation for everyone who believes, for the Jew first and also for the Greek."

5. Does the message of Jesus' dying on the cross seem foolish to you?

1 Corinthians 1:18 –
>"For the message of the cross is foolishness to those who are perishing, but to us who are being saved it is the power of God."

REPENTANCE

1. Are you preparing your heart each morning for repentance?

Psalm 51:1-2 –
>"Have mercy upon me, O God,
>According to Your lovingkindness;
>According to the multitude of Your tender mercies,
>Blot out my transgressions.
>Wash me thoroughly from my iniquity,
>And cleanse me from my sin."

Psalm 139:23-24 –
>"Search me, O God, and know my heart;
>Try me, and know my anxieties;
>And see if *there is any* wicked way in me,
>And lead me in the way everlasting."

2. Have you not only believed but repented, turning from your sin?

Matthew 4:17 –
>"From that time Jesus began to preach and to say, 'Repent, for the kingdom of heaven is at hand.'"

Acts 2:38 –
>"Then Peter said to them, 'Repent, and let every one of you be baptized in the name of Jesus Christ for the remission of sins; and you shall receive the gift of the Holy Spirit.'"

Acts 26:20 –
>"…they should repent, turn to God, and do works befitting repentance."

3. Do your good works show others that you are truly repentant?

Ephesians 2:10 –
>"For we are His workmanship, created in Christ Jesus for good works, which God prepared beforehand that we should walk in them."

4. Do you turn from sin because of God's goodness or do you just assume it doesn't bother Him?

Romans 2:4 –
>"Or do you despise the riches of His goodness, forbearance, and longsuffering, not knowing that the goodness of God leads you to repentance?"

5. Do you realize that if you have died to sin you could not possibly live like you used to?

Romans 6:1 –
   "What shall we say then? Shall we continue in sin that grace may abound?"

Romans 6:2 –
   "Certainly not! How shall we who died to sin live any longer in it?"

Ephesians 2:1-3 –
   "And you *He made alive*, who were dead in trespasses and sins, in which you once walked according to the course of this world, according to the prince of the power of the air, the spirit who now works in the sons of disobedience, among whom also we all once conducted ourselves in the lusts of our flesh, fulfilling the desires of the flesh and of the mind, and were by nature children of wrath, just as the others."

6. When you sin, are you sorry for the moment or does your sorrow lead you to truly repent?

1 Corinthians 7:9 –
   "Now I rejoice, not that you were made sorry, but that your sorrow led to repentance. For you were made sorry in a godly manner, that you might suffer loss from us in nothing. For godly sorrow produces repentance leading to salvation, not to be regretted; but the sorrow of the world produces death."

PHONY OR GENUINE?

1. Do you receive Jesus humbly and poor in spirit, knowing you are nothing without Him or do you feel you are doing God a

favor by believing in Him?

Matthew 5:3 –
> **"Blessed are the poor in spirit, for theirs is the kingdom of heaven."**

2. Are you proud of yourself for doing things for God or do you humbly realize that you are only doing these things because He is working through you?

2 Corinthians 3:4-5 –
> **"And we have such trust through Christ toward God. Not that we are sufficient of ourselves to think of anything as being from ourselves, but our sufficiency is from God"**

3. Do you take credit for any results that come from sharing your faith?

1 Corinthians 3:6-7 –
> **I planted, Apollos watered, but God gave the increase. 7 So then neither he who plants is anything, nor he who waters, but God who gives the increase.**

4. Do you feel that you are wise in this world?

1 Corinthians 3:18-20 –
> **"Let no one deceive himself. If anyone among you seems to be wise in this age, let him become a fool that he may become wise. For the wisdom of this world is foolishness with God. For it is written, 'He catches the wise in their own craftiness;' and again, 'The LORD knows the thoughts of the wise, that they are futile.'"**

WILLINGNESS TO CHANGE

1. Do you understand that God hates pride, religion, and arrogance? God only wants people who are willing to be humble.

Luke 18:11-14 –
 "The Pharisee stood and prayed thus with himself, 'God, I thank You that I am not like other men—extortioners, unjust, adulterers, or even as this tax collector. I fast twice a week; I give tithes of all that I possess.' And the tax collector, standing afar off, would not so much as raise his eyes to heaven, but beat his breast, saying, 'God, be merciful to me a sinner!' I tell you, this man went down to his house justified rather than the other; for everyone who exalts himself will be humbled, and he who humbles himself will be exalted."

John 3:30 –
 "He must increase, but I *must* decrease.

2. Do you walk away from sinful lifestyles? After becoming a Christian, has your lifestyle changed? Are you still spending time with those who spiritually bring you down?

John 8:10-11 –
 "When Jesus had raised Himself up and saw no one but the woman, He said to her, 'Woman, where are those accusers of yours? Has no one condemned you?' She said, 'No one, Lord.' And Jesus said to her, 'Neither do I condemn you; GO AND SIN NOT MORE.'" (Emphasis added.)

1 John 1:3-6 –
 "...that which we have seen and heard we declare to you, that you also may have fellowship with us; and truly our fellowship *is* with the Father and with His Son Jesus Christ. And these things we write to you that your joy

may be full. This is the message which we have heard from Him and declare to you, that God is light and in Him is no darkness at all. If we say that we have fellowship with Him, and walk in darkness, we lie and do not practice the truth."

1 Corinthians 6:9-10 –

"Do you not know that the unrighteous will not inherit the kingdom of God? Do not be deceived. Neither fornicators, nor idolaters, nor adulterers, nor homosexuals, nor sodomites, nor thieves, nor covetous, nor drunkards, nor revilers, nor extortioners will inherit the kingdom of God."

1 Corinthians 15:33-34 –

"Do not be deceived: 'Evil company corrupts good habits.' Awake to righteousness, and do not sin; for some do not have the knowledge of God. I speak this to your shame."

3. Do you know that when you became a Christian you became a new person, reconciled to God? Are you putting off your old way of life?

2 Corinthians 5:17-19 –

"Therefore, if anyone is in Christ, he is a new creation; old things have passed away; behold, all things have become new. Now all things are of God, who has reconciled us to Himself through Jesus Christ, and has given us the ministry of reconciliation, that is, that God was in Christ reconciling the world to Himself, not imputing their trespasses to them, and has committed to us the word of reconciliation."

Ephesians 4:20-24 –

"But you have not so learned Christ, if indeed you have heard Him and have been taught by Him, as the truth is in Jesus: that you put off, concerning your former conduct, the old man which grows corrupt according to the deceitful lusts, and be renewed in the spirit of your mind, and that you put on the new man which was created according to God, in true righteousness and holiness."

Colossians 3:5-10 –
"Therefore put to death your members which are on the earth: fornication, uncleanness, passion, evil desire, and covetousness, which is idolatry. Because of these things the wrath of God is coming upon the sons of disobedience, in which you yourselves once walked when you lived in them. But now you yourselves are to put off all these: anger, wrath, malice, blasphemy, filthy language out of your mouth. Do not lie to one another, since you have put off the old man with his deeds, and have put on the new *man* who is renewed in knowledge according to the image of Him who created him…."

4. Are you careful how you talk?

Ephesians 4:29 –
"Let no corrupt word proceed out of your mouth, but what is good for necessary edification, that it may impart grace to the hearers."

Colossians 3:16-17 –
"Let the word of Christ dwell in you richly in all wisdom, teaching and admonishing one another in psalms and hymns and spiritual songs, singing with grace in your hearts to the Lord. And *whatever* you do in word or deed, *do* all in the name of the Lord Jesus, giving thanks to God the Father through Him."

Ephesians 4:25 –
"Therefore, putting away lying, 'Let each one of you speak truth with his neighbor,' for we are members of one another."

5. Are you having sex before marriage?

Ephesians 5:3 –
>"But fornication and all uncleanness or covetousness, let it not even be named among you, as is fitting for saints."

6. Are you a bitter person?

Ephesians 4:31-32 –
>"Let all bitterness, wrath, anger, clamor, and evil speaking be put away from you, with all malice. And be kind to one another, tenderhearted, forgiving one another, just as God in Christ forgave you."

7. Do you realize that as a Christian you are truly a child and heir of God?

Galatians 3:26, 29 –
>"For you are all sons of God through faith in Christ Jesus. And if you are Christ's, then you are Abraham's seed, and heirs according to the promise."

Galatians 4:5-7 –
>"...to redeem those who were under the law, that we might receive the adoption as sons. 6 And because you are sons, God has sent forth the Spirit of His Son into your hearts, crying out, "Abba, Father!" 7 Therefore you are no longer a slave but a son, and if a son, then an heir of God through Christ."

8. Do you realize that before you were a Christian you were completely dead in your sin and that God is the one who made you alive?

Ephesians 2:1, 4, 8 –
>1 "And you He made alive, who were dead in trespasses and sins..."

> **4 "But God, who is rich in mercy, because of His great love with which He loved us...."
> 8 "For by grace you have been saved through faith, and that not of yourselves; it is the gift of God..."**

9. Do you understand that once you become a Christian that you need to walk in your new life? Do you see that your new life needs to look different?

Romans 6:4 –
> **"...just as Christ was raised from the dead by the glory of the Father, even so we also should walk in newness of life."**

10. Do you see that your life has to change so that you are not conformed to the world anymore?

Romans 12:2 –
> **"And do not be conformed to this world, but be transformed by the renewing of your mind, that you may prove what is that good and acceptable and perfect will of God."**

11. Do you realize that when you become a Christian, the Holy Spirit lives in you?

1 Corinthians 3:16 –
> **"Do you not know that you are the temple of God and that the Spirit of God dwells in you?"**

PRIORITIES – WHO'S THE BOSS NOW?

1. Is your treasure found in this world? Is your job, hobby, friends or family more important than your relationship with Jesus?

Matthew 6:21 –
> "For where your treasure is, there your heart will be also."

Matthew 6:24 –
> "No one can serve two masters; for either he will hate the one and love the other, or else he will be loyal to the one and despise the other. You cannot serve God and mammon."

Matthew 6:33 –
> "But seek FIRST the kingdom of God and His righteousness, and all these things shall be added to you." (Emphasis ours.)

Matthew 10:37 –
> "He who loves father or mother more than Me is not worthy of Me. And he who loves son or daughter more than me is not worthy of Me."

2. Do you understand that you must love the Lord with all of your heart, soul, and mind over everything else in your life?

Matthew 22:36-37 –
> "'Teacher, which is the great commandment in the law?' Jesus said to him, 'You shall love the LORD your God with all your heart, with all your soul, and with all your mind.'"

3. Do you understand that God is not interested in how much we have, but what is in our hearts to give?

Luke 21:1-4 –
> "And He looked up and saw the rich putting their gifts into the treasury, and He saw also a certain poor widow putting in two mites. So He said, 'Truly I say to you that this poor widow has put in more than all; for all these

out of their abundance have put in offerings for God, but she out of her poverty put in all the livelihood that she had.'"

4. Do you understand that as a Christian you set your mind on the things of God, not the things of this world?

Romans 8:5, 9, 12 –
5 "For those who live according to the flesh set their minds on the things of the flesh, but those who live according to the Spirit, the things of the Spirit."
9 "But you are not in the flesh but in the Spirit, if indeed the Spirit of God dwells in you. Now if anyone does not have the Spirit of Christ, he is not His."
12 "But you are not in the flesh but in the Spirit, if indeed the Spirit of God dwells in you. Now if anyone does not have the Spirit of Christ, he is not His."

5. Do you see that to be a Christian means that you live your life for the Lord and not for yourself?

Romans 14:7 –
"For none of us lives to himself, and no one dies to himself."

6. Do you do everything in your life (work, hobbies, family) to the glory of God? Is your life being used in all of these areas to serve Him?

1 Corinthians 10:31 –
"Therefore, whether you eat or drink, or whatever you do, do all to the glory of God."

7. Do you spend your time trying to please men or please God?

Galatians 1:10 –
"For do I now persuade men, or God? Or do I seek to

please men? For if I still pleased men, I would not be a bondservant of Christ."

OBEDIENCE – JUST DO IT!

1. Do you understand that the only people who are truly Christians are those who don't just say they believe, but they actually do what God calls them to do?

Matthew 7:21, 24, 26 –
> **21 "Not everyone who says to Me, 'Lord, Lord,' shall enter the kingdom of heaven, but he who does the will of My Father in heaven."**
> **24 "Therefore whoever hears these sayings of Mine, and does them, I will liken him to a wise man who built his house on the rock."**
> **26 "Therefore whoever hears these sayings of Mine, and does them, I will liken him to a wise man who built his house on the rock."**

2. Do you see when Jesus touches someone's life, the natural response is to follow Him?

Matthew 20:34 –
> **"So Jesus had compassion and touched their eyes. And immediately their eyes received sight, and they followed Him."**

3. Do you understand that being a Christian means doing things for God—not to be saved, but because you are saved? This should be a natural response.

Matthew 25:34-40 –
> **"Then the King will say to those on His right hand, 'Come, you blessed of My Father, inherit the kingdom prepared for you from the foundation of the world: for I**

was hungry and you gave Me food; I was thirsty and you gave Me drink; I was a stranger and you took Me in; I was naked and you clothed Me; I was sick and you visited Me; I was in prison and you came to Me.' Then the righteous will answer Him, saying, 'Lord, when did we see You hungry and feed You, or thirsty and give You drink? When did we see You a stranger and take You in, or naked and clothe You? Or when did we see You sick, or in prison, and come to You?' And the King will answer and say to them, 'Assuredly, I say to you, inasmuch as you did it to one of the least of these My brethren, you did it to Me.'"

Romans 2:6-9 –
"...who 'will render to each one according to his deeds:' eternal life to those who by patient continuance in doing good seek for glory, honor, and immortality; but to those who are self-seeking and do not obey the truth, but obey unrighteousness—indignation and wrath, tribulation and anguish, on every soul of man who does evil..."

4. Do you understand that being a Christian means having a changed lifestyle? The things we used to do, we would not consider doing anymore. We live in God's economy now, not the world's.

Luke 19:8-10 –
"Then Zacchaeus stood and said to the Lord, 'Look, Lord, I give half of my goods to the poor; and if I have taken anything from anyone by false accusation, I restore fourfold.' And Jesus said to him, 'Today salvation has come to this house, because he also is a son of Abraham; for the Son of Man has come to seek and to save that which was lost.'"

5. Do you understand that your body is now to be used as an instrument of good things to God instead of how you used to live?

Romans 6:12, 18-19, 22 –
>12 "Therefore do not let sin reign in your mortal body, that you should obey it in its lusts."
>18-19 "And having been set free from sin, you became slaves of righteousness. I speak in human terms because of the weakness of your flesh. For just as you presented your members as slaves of uncleanness, and of lawlessness leading to more lawlessness, so now present your members as slaves of righteousness for holiness."
>22 "But now having been set free from sin, and having become slaves of God, you have your fruit to holiness, and the end, everlasting life."

6. Do you see that your Christianity is something that is acted out in your life?

Romans 12:9-13
>"Let love be without hypocrisy. Abhor what is evil. Cling to what is good. Be kindly affectionate to one another with brotherly love, in honor giving preference to one another; not lagging in diligence, fervent in spirit, serving the Lord; rejoicing in hope, patient in tribulation, continuing steadfastly in prayer; distributing to the needs of the saints, given to hospitality."

Romans 13:12
>"The night is far spent, the day is at hand. Therefore let us cast off the works of darkness, and let us put on the armor of light."

7. Do you abide in His Word, which means to comply with what He says?

John 8:31 –
>"Then Jesus said to those Jews who believed Him, 'If you abide in My word, you are My disciples indeed.'"

8. Have you given up your life to whatever God asks of you?

John 12:25 –
> "He who loves his life will lose it, and he who hates his life in this world will keep it for eternal life."

9. Do you keep God's commandments, which in turn shows that you do love Him? Do you understand that if you do not keep God's Word, then you really don't love Him?

John 14:15, 21, 23-24 –
> **15** "If you love Me, keep My commandments."
> **21** "He who has My commandments and keeps them, it is he who loves Me. And he who loves Me will be loved by My Father, and I will love him and manifest Myself to him."
> **23-24** "Jesus answered and said to him, 'If anyone loves Me, he will keep My word; and My Father will love him, and We will come to him and make Our home with him. He who does not love Me does not keep My words; and the word which you hear is not Mine but the Father's who sent Me.'"

10. Are you a faithful servant of Christ?

1 Corinthians 4:1-2 –
> "Let a man so consider us, as servants of Christ and stewards of the mysteries of God. Moreover it is required in stewards that one be found faithful."

11. Do you understand that the Christian life is a race to be run?

1 Corinthians 9:24-27 –
> "Do you not know that those who run in a race all run, but one receives the prize? Run in such a way that you may obtain it. And everyone who competes for the prize is temperate in all things. Now they do it to obtain a

perishable crown, but we for an imperishable crown. Therefore I run thus: not with uncertainty. Thus I fight: not as one who beats the air. But I discipline my body and bring it into subjection, lest, when I have preached to others, I myself should become disqualified."

12. Are you living by things you see in this world or by what you cannot see?

2 Corinthians 4:16-18 –
"Therefore we do not lose heart. Even though our outward man is perishing, yet the inward man is being renewed day by day. For our light affliction, which is but for a moment, is working for us a far more exceeding and eternal weight of glory, while we do not look at the things which are seen, but at the things which are not seen. For the things which are seen are temporary, but the things which are not seen are eternal."

2 Corinthians 5:7 –
"For we walk by faith, not by sight."

13. Do you give cheerfully out of your heart?

2 Corinthians 9:6-7 –
"But this I say: He who sows sparingly will also reap sparingly, and he who sows bountifully will also reap bountifully. So let each one give as he purposes in his heart, not grudgingly or of necessity; for God loves a cheerful giver."

14. Do you realize that you were created for good works and that your life here has a purpose?

Ephesians 2:10 –
> "For we are His workmanship, created in Christ Jesus for good works, which God prepared beforehand that we should walk in them."

15. How do you deal with anger?

Ephesians 4:26 –
> "'Be angry, and do not sin: do not let the sun go down on your wrath,' nor give place to the devil."

16. Do you steal?

Ephesians 4:28 –
> "Let him who stole steal no longer, but rather let him labor, working with his hands what is good, that he may have something to give him who has need."

17. Do you imitate God?

Ephesians 5:1-2 –
> "Therefore be imitators of God as dear children. And walk in love, as Christ also has loved us and given Himself for us, an offering and a sacrifice to God for a sweet-smelling aroma."

18. Are you wise?

Ephesians 5:15-17 –
> "See then that you walk circumspectly, not as fools but as wise, redeeming the time, because the days are evil. Therefore do not be unwise, but understand what the will of the Lord is."

WHAT'S IT GOING TO COST ME?

1. Are you one of those people who talk about God and are very religious and yet your heart is far from Him?

Matthew 15:8 –
> **"'These people draw near to Me with their mouth, and honor Me with their lips,
> But their heart is far from Me. And in vain they worship Me, teaching as doctrines the commandments of men.'"**

2. Do you walk in light and not darkness?

John 8:12 –
> **"Then Jesus spoke to them again, saying, 'I am the light of the world. He who follows Me shall not walk in darkness, but have the light of life.'"**

3. Do you see that a person can know about God and yet not be a Christian?

Romans 1:21 –
> **"...because, although they knew God, they did not glorify Him as God, nor were thankful, but became futile in their thoughts, and their foolish hearts were darkened."**

4. Do you understand that to be a Christian means you are led by God?

Romans 8:14 –
> **"For as many as are led by the Spirit of God, these are sons of God."**

5. Do you examine yourself to make sure you are truly a Christian?

2 Corinthians 13:5 –
> "Examine yourselves as to whether you are in the faith. Test yourselves. Do you not know yourselves, that Jesus Christ is in you?—unless indeed you are disqualified."

6. Do you realize that being a Christian means following the narrow way and that there is a cost to following Christ?

Matthew 7:13-14 –
> "Enter by the narrow gate; for wide is the gate and broad is the way that leads to destruction, and there are many who go in by it. Because narrow is the gate and difficult is the way which leads to life, and there are few who find it."

Matthew 8:19-22 –
> "Then a certain scribe came and said to Him, 'Teacher, I will follow You wherever You go.' And Jesus said to him, 'Foxes have holes and birds of the air have nests, but the Son of Man has nowhere to lay His head.' Then another of His disciples said to Him, 'Lord, let me first go and bury my father.' But Jesus said to him, 'Follow Me, and let the dead bury their own dead.'"

7. Do you understand that being a Christian takes endurance until the end and people will not always like you because of your belief in Christ?

Matthew 10:22, 32-33 –
> 22 "And you will be hated by all for My name's sake. But he who endures to the end will be saved."
> 32-33 "Therefore whoever confesses Me before men, him I will also confess before My Father who is in heaven. But whoever denies Me before men, him I will also deny before My Father who is in heaven."

8. Do you understand that to be a Christian means losing your life

Sincerely His

and giving it up to Christ for Him to use for His purposes? It is like finding a treasure and then giving up everything for that treasure.

Matthew 10:39 –
> "He who finds his life will lose it, and he who loses his life for My sake will find it."

Matthew 13: 44-45 –
> "Again, the kingdom of heaven is like treasure hidden in a field, which a man found and hid; and for joy over it he goes and sells all that he has and buys that field.
> Again, the kingdom of heaven is like a merchant seeking beautiful pearls, who, when he had found one pearl of great price, went and sold all that he had and bought it."

Matthew 16:24-26 –
> "Then Jesus said to His disciples, 'If anyone desires to come after Me, let him deny himself, and take up his cross, and follow Me. For whoever desires to save his life will lose it, but whoever loses his life for My sake will find it. For what profit is it to a man if he gains the whole world, and loses his own soul? Or what will a man give in exchange for his soul?'"

BEARING FRUIT

1. Does your life bear fruit?

Matthew 3:8, 10 –
> 8 "Therefore bear fruits worthy of repentance..."
> 10 "And even now the ax is laid to the root of the trees. Therefore every tree which does not bear good fruit is cut down and thrown into the fire."

2. Is your Christian walk seen by others as salt and light?

Matthew 5:13-14, 16 –
> **13-14 "You are the salt of the earth; but if the salt loses its flavor, how shall it be seasoned? It is then good for nothing but to be thrown out and trampled underfoot by men. You are the light of the world. A city that is set on a hill cannot be hidden."**
> **16 "Let your light so shine before men, that they may see your good works and glorify your Father in heaven."**

3. Do you realize that how we conduct our lives shows people if we are truly Christians?

Matthew 12:33, 50 –
> **33 "Let your light so shine before men, that they may see your good works and glorify your Father in heaven."**
> **50 "For whoever does the will of My Father in heaven is My brother and sister and mother."**

4. Do you realize that if you accepted Christ at one point in your life and it became difficult and you walked away, that you might not be a Christian? Do you realize that in order to know if you are a Christian means you will be able to tell by your fruit?

Matthew 13:20-23 –
> **"But he who received the seed on stony places, this is he who hears the word and immediately receives it with joy; yet he has no root in himself, but endures only for a while. For when tribulation or persecution arises because of the word, immediately he stumbles. Now he who received seed among the thorns is he who hears the word, and the cares of this world and the deceitfulness of riches choke the word, and he becomes unfruitful. But he who received seed on the good ground is he who hears the word and understands it, who indeed bears fruit and produces: some a hundredfold, some sixty, some thirty."**

John 15:1-2, 6, 14 –
>1-2 "I am the true vine, and My Father is the vinedresser. Every branch in Me that does not bear fruit He takes away; and every branch that bears fruit He prunes, that it may bear more fruit."
>6 "If anyone does not abide in Me, he is cast out as a branch and is withered; and they gather them and throw them into the fire, and they are burned."
>14 "If anyone does not abide in Me, he is cast out as a branch and is withered; and they gather them and throw them into the fire, and they are burned."

5. Does your life reflect a life worthy of the calling of God?

Ephesians 4:1-2 –
>"I, therefore, the prisoner of the Lord, beseech you to walk worthy of the calling with which you were called, with all lowliness and gentleness, with longsuffering, bearing with one another in love...."

6. Have you examined yourself to see if your life has evidence of the fruit of the Spirit?

Galatians 5:19-22 –
>"Now the works of the flesh are evident, which are: adultery, fornication, uncleanness, lewdness, idolatry, sorcery, hatred, contentions, jealousies, outbursts of wrath, selfish ambitions, dissensions, heresies, envy, murders, drunkenness, revelries, and the like; of which I tell you beforehand, just as I also told you in time past, that those who practice such things will not inherit the kingdom of God. But the fruit of the Spirit is love, joy, peace, longsuffering, kindness, goodness, faithfulness, gentleness, self-control. Against such there is no law."

SHARE THE GOOD NEWS WITH OTHERS

1. Do you see that when Jesus comes into someone's life that the natural response is to tell people?

Mark 5:19 –
>"However, Jesus did not permit him, but said to him, 'Go home to your friends, and tell them what great things the Lord has done for you, and how He has had compassion on you.'"

2. Are you bold in sharing Christ with others?

Acts 4:13 –
>"Now when they saw the boldness of Peter and John, and perceived that they were uneducated and untrained men, they marveled. And they realized that they had been with Jesus."

3. Do you feel compelled to share Christ?

Acts 4:19-20 –
>"But Peter and John answered and said to them, 'Whether it is right in the sight of God to listen to you more than to God, you judge. FOR WE CANNOT BUT SPEAK the things which we have seen and heard.'" (Emphasis ours.)

4. Are you a sweet fragrance of salvation to people?

2 Corinthians 2:15-16 –
>"For we are to God the fragrance of Christ among those who are being saved and among those who are perishing. To the one we are the aroma of death leading to death, and to the other the aroma of life leading to life."

5. Is your life so transformed that people know you are a Christian?

Acts 3: 2-3 –
>"You are our epistle written in our hearts, known and read by all men; clearly you are an epistle of Christ, ministered by us, written not with ink but by the Spirit of the living God, not on tablets of stone but on tablets of flesh, that is, of the heart."

FIND YOUR IDENTITY GROUP

1. Do you see how important that going to church, praying and taking communion is, and that this must be done regularly?

Acts. 2:42 –
>"And they continued steadfastly in the apostles' doctrine and fellowship, in the breaking of bread, and in prayers."

Hebrews 10:25 -
>"Not forsaking the assembling of ourselves together, as the manner of some *is*; but exhorting *one another*: and so much the more, as ye see the day approaching."

2. Do you expose those things that are wrong?

Ephesians 5:11 –
>"And have no fellowship with the unfruitful works of darkness, but rather expose them."

3. Do you look after the needs of your fellow Christians?

Ephesians 4:1-6 –
>"I, therefore, the prisoner of the Lord, beseech you to walk worthy of the calling with which you were called, with all lowliness and gentleness, with longsuffering,

bearing with one another in love, endeavoring to keep the unity of the Spirit in the bond of peace. There *is* one body and one Spirit, just as you were called in one hope of your calling; one Lord, one faith, one baptism; one God and Father of all, who *is* above all, and through all, and in you all."

4. Are you cultivating harmonious relationships among fellow believers?

1 John 2:7-11 –
"Brethren, I write no new commandment to you, but an old commandment which you have had from the beginning. The old commandment is the word which you heard from the beginning. Again, a new commandment I write to you, which thing is true in Him and in you, because the darkness is passing away, and the true light is already shining. He who says he is in the light, and hates his brother, is in darkness until now. He who loves his brother abides in the light, and there is no cause for stumbling in him. But he who hates his brother is in darkness and walks in darkness, and does not know where he is going, because the darkness has blinded his eyes."

Our hope and prayer is that this book will help you examine your own life to see if you are "Sincerely His." – Rob and Lisa
www.robertslaizure.com

Printed in the United States
22708LVS00005B/190-510